The Art Of Mandalas Coloring Book

Creative Time With Mandalas Coloring Book

Mandala Coloring Book

By : Gala Publication

Published By :

Gala Publication

ISBN-13: **978-1522707813**
ISBN-10: **1522707816**

Design 1

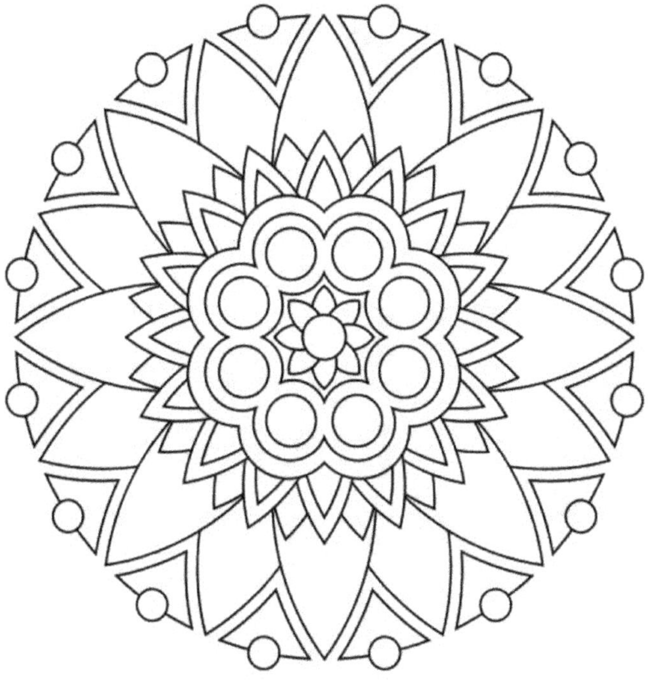

Design 2

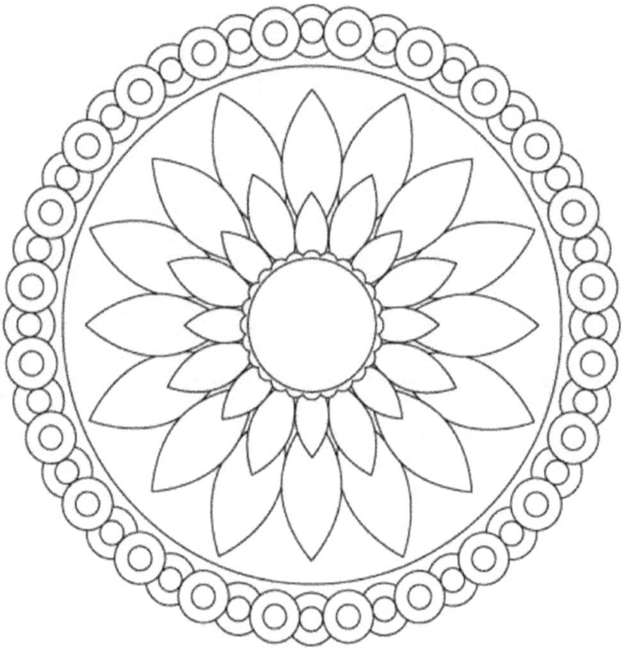

Design 3

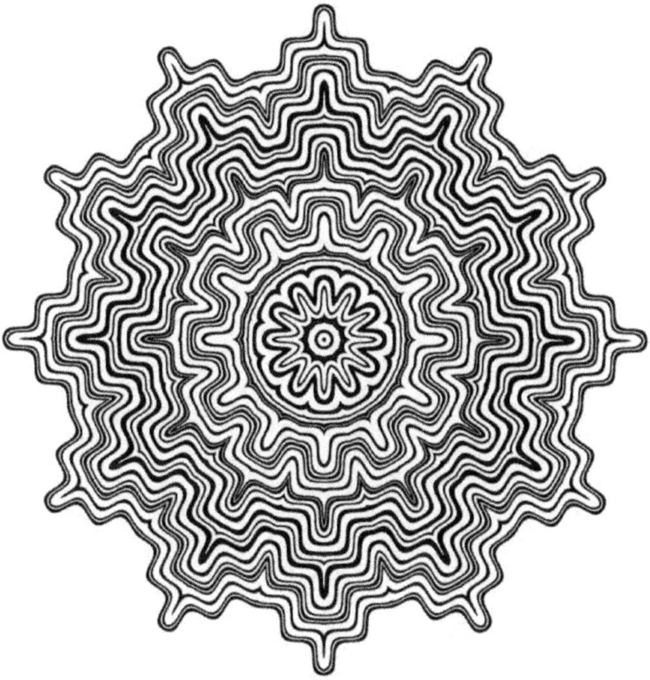

Design 4

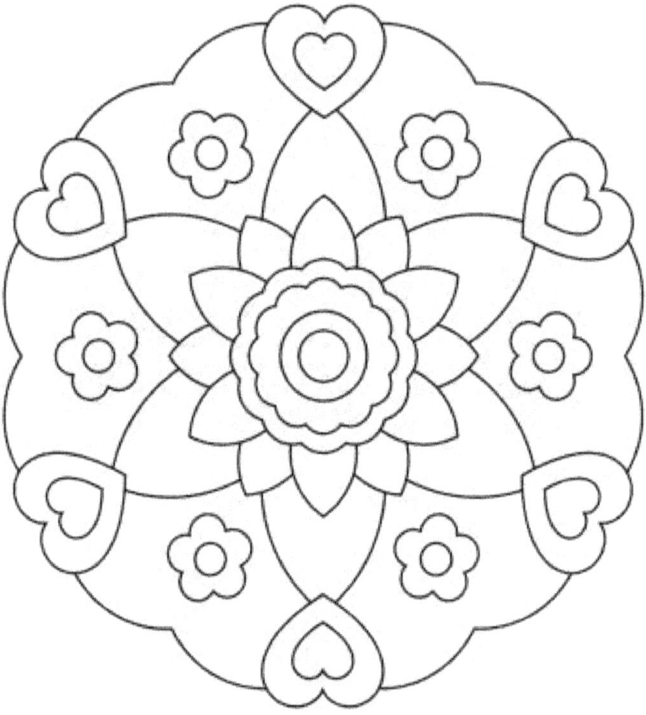

Design 5

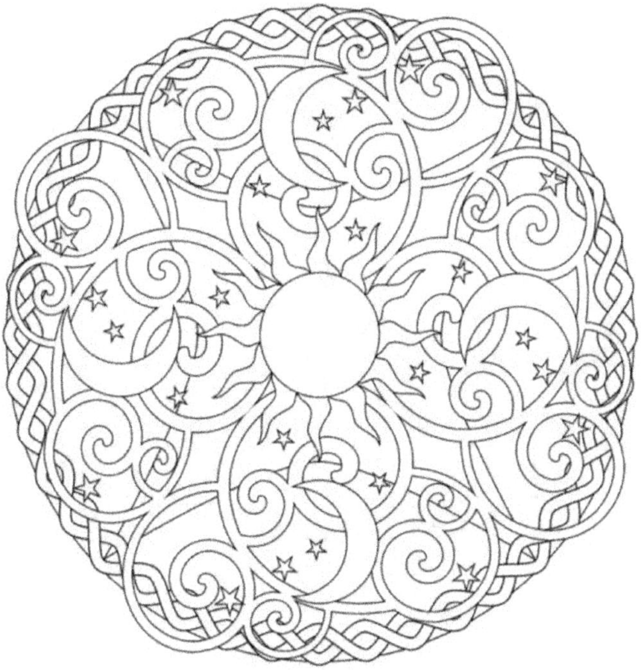

Design 6

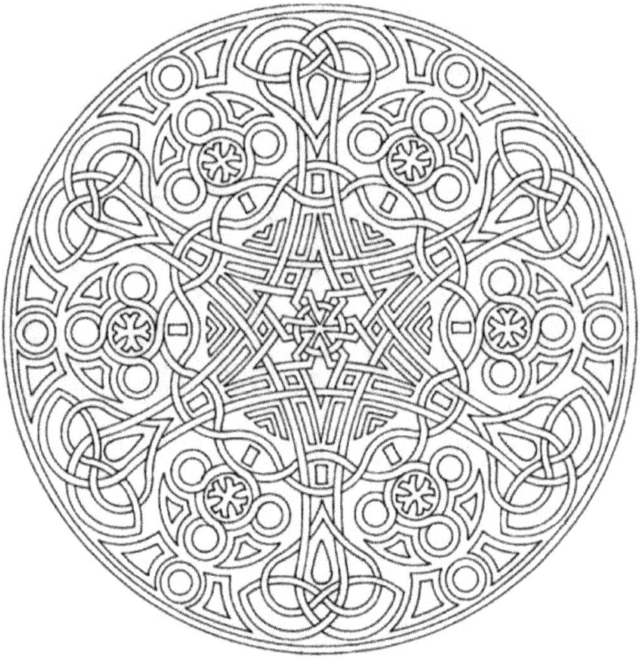

Design 7

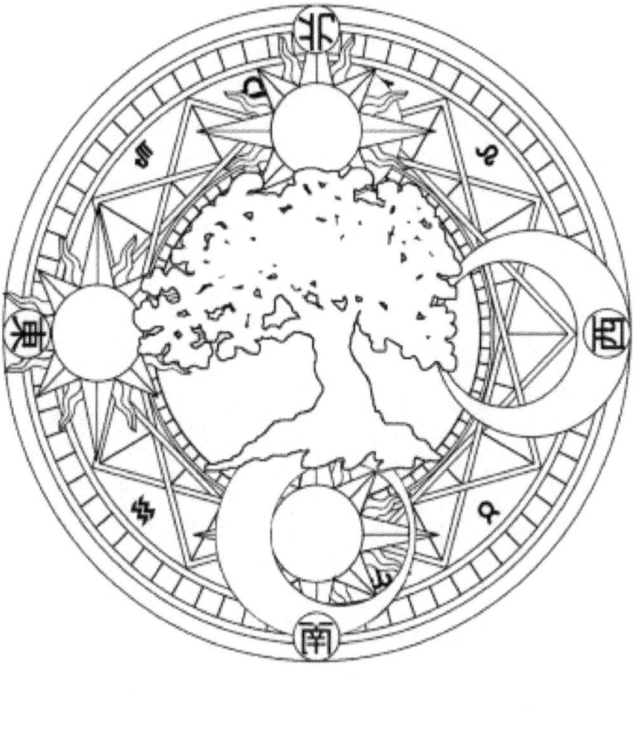

Design 8

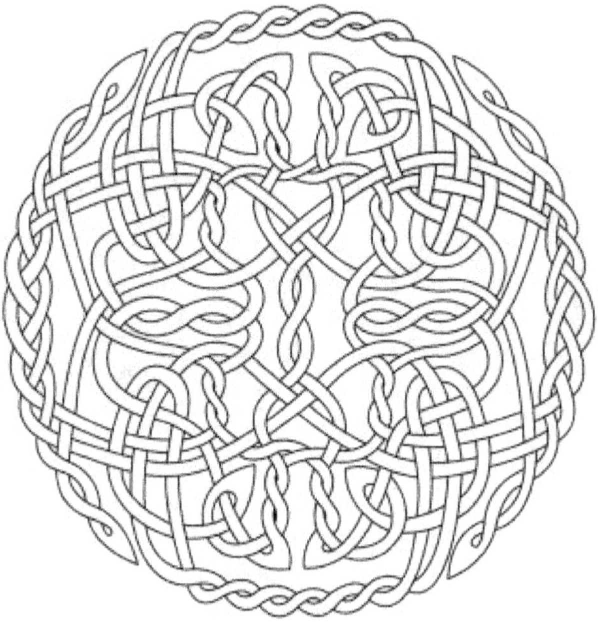

Design 9

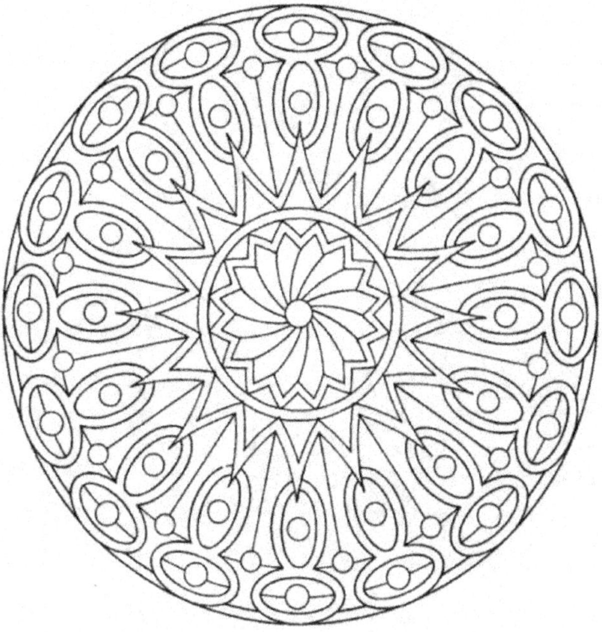

Design 10

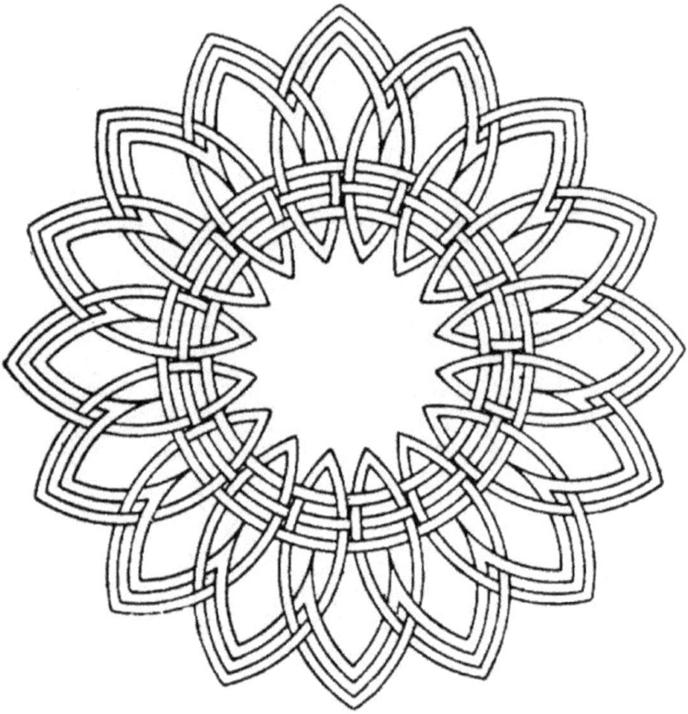

Design 11

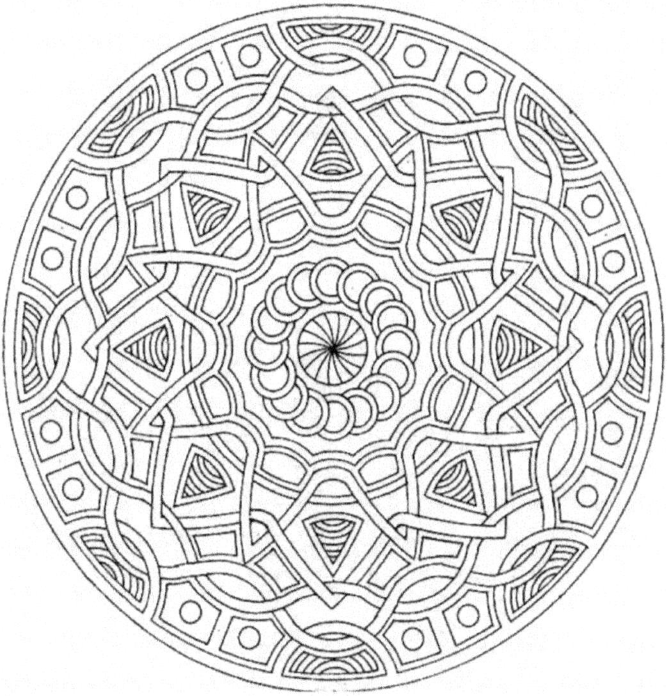

Design 12

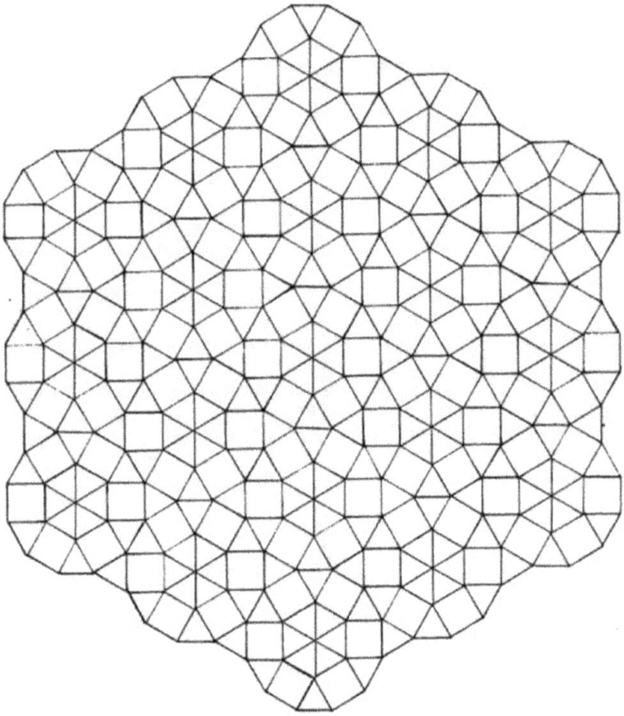

Design 13

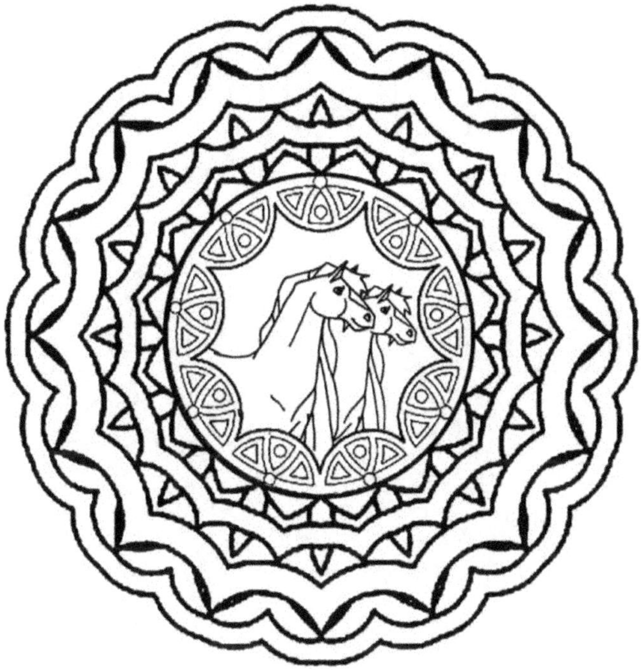

Design 14

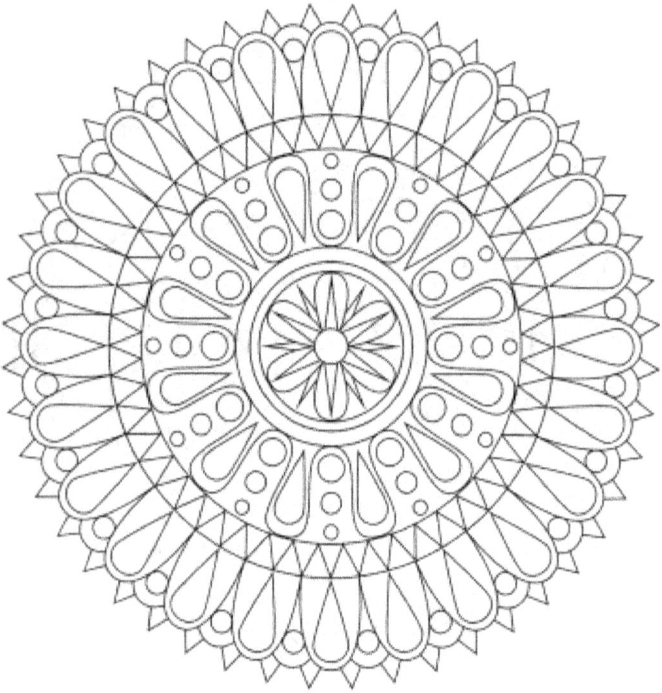

Design 15

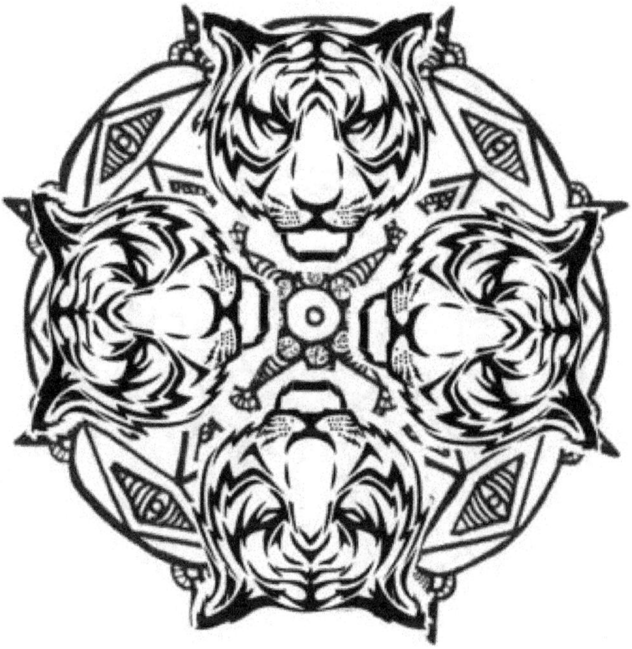

Design 16

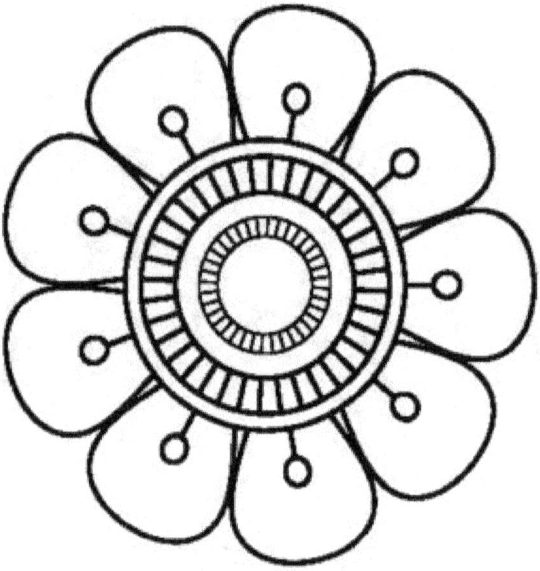

Design 17

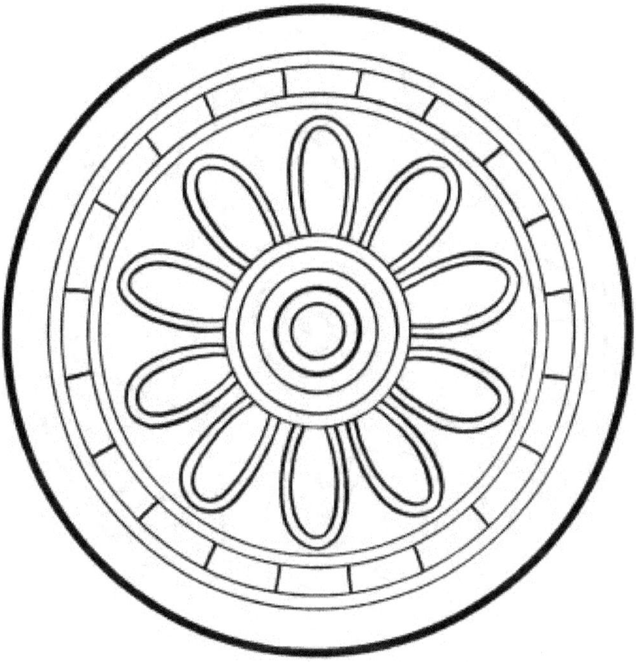

Design 18

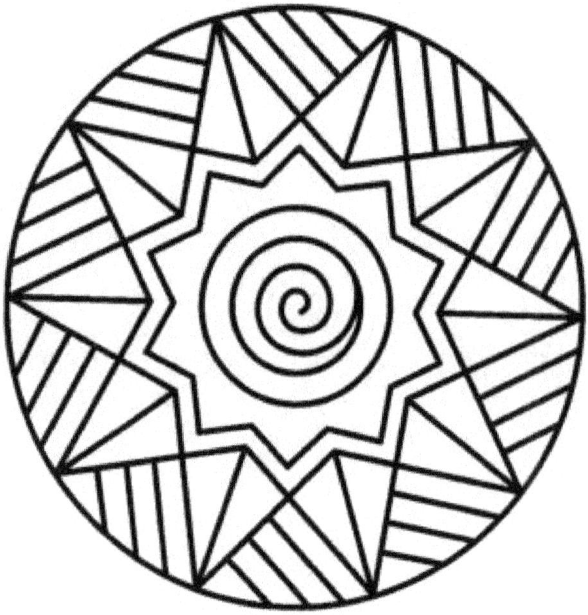

Design 19

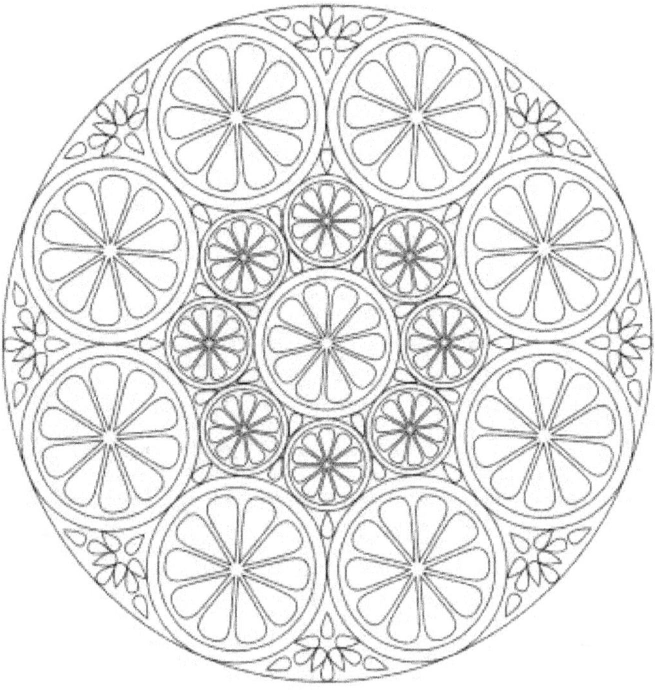

Design 20

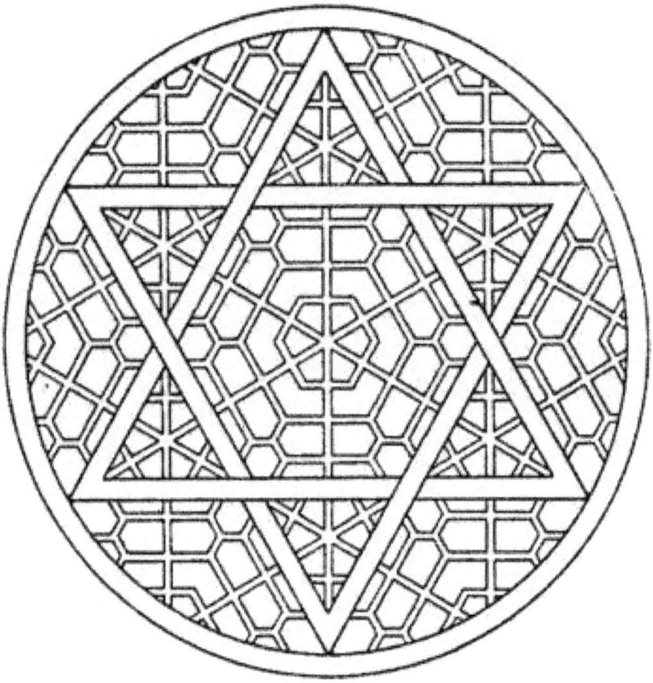

Design 21

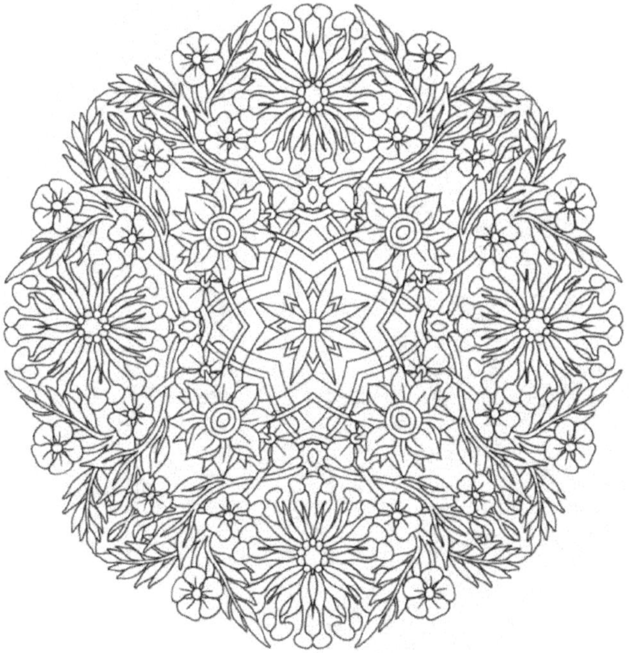

Design 22

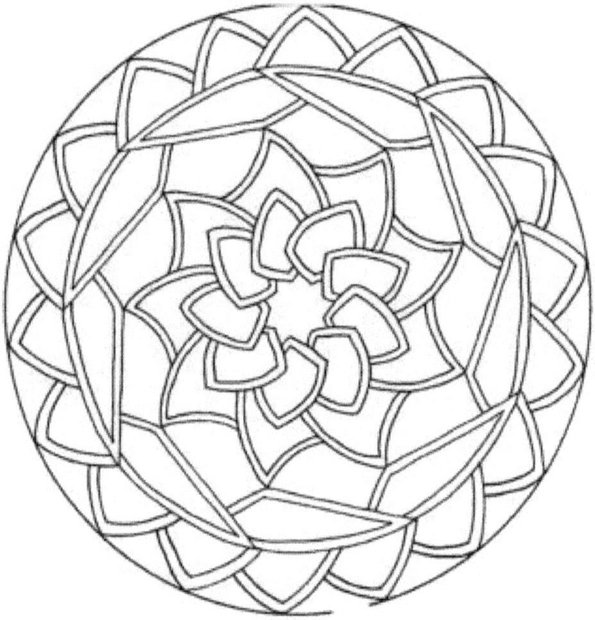

Design 23

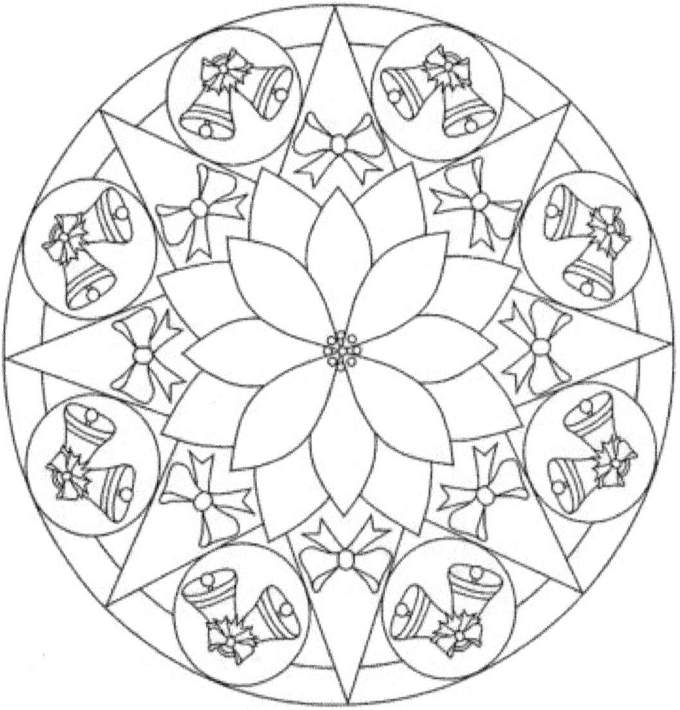

Design 24

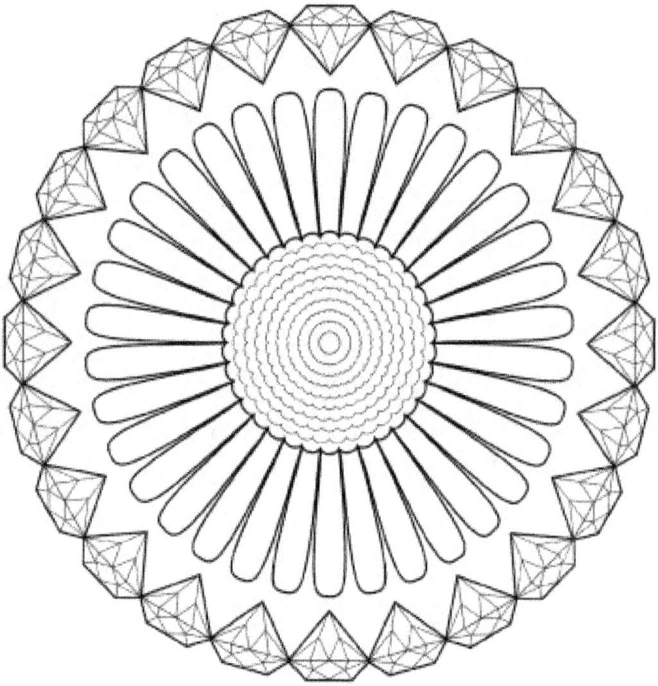

Design 25

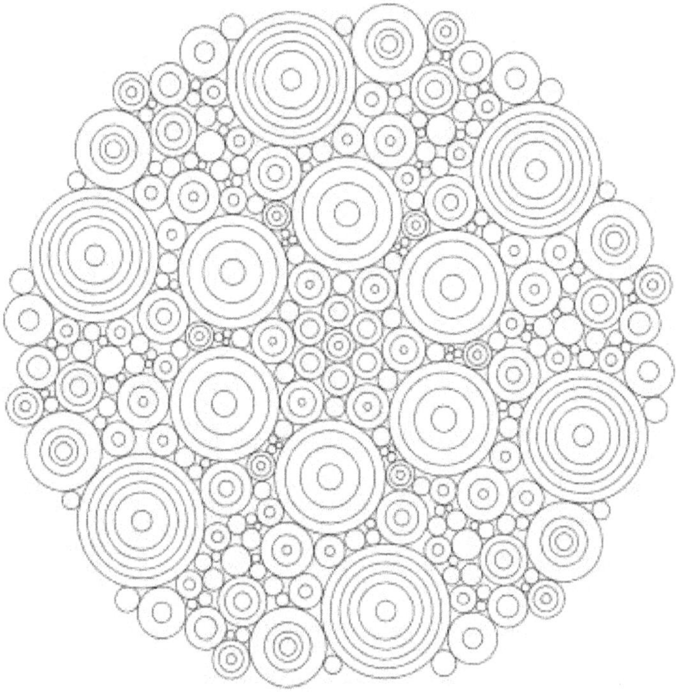

Design 26

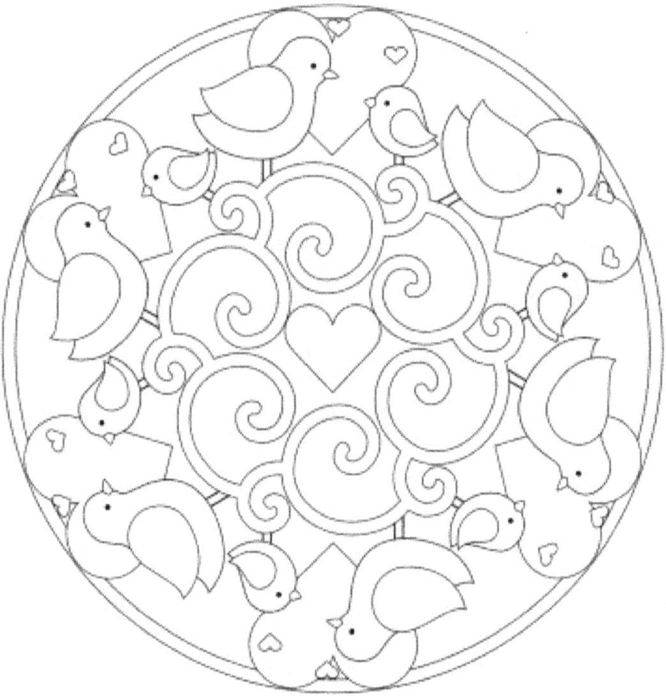

Design 27

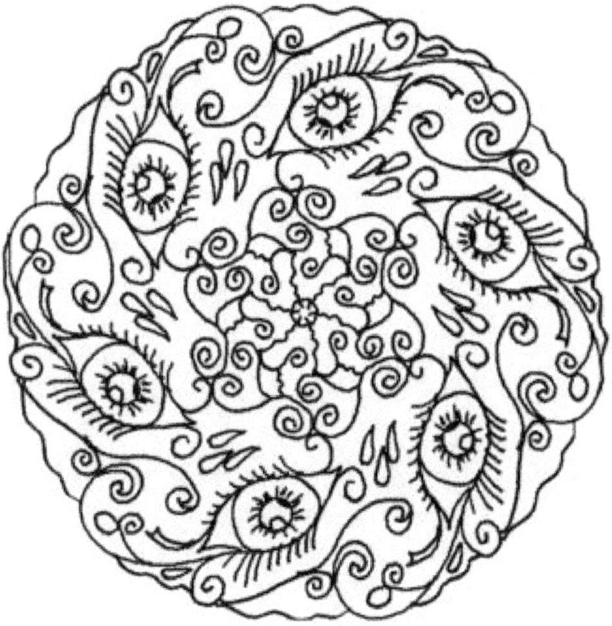

Design 28

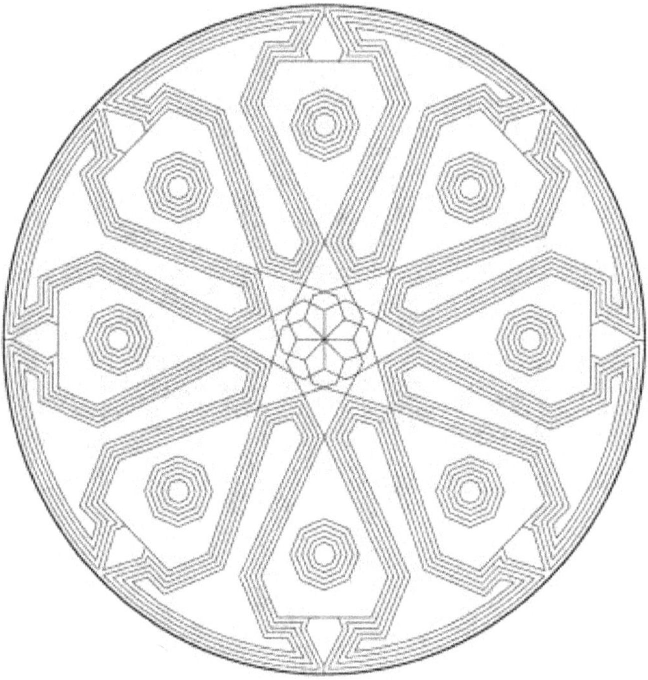

Design 29

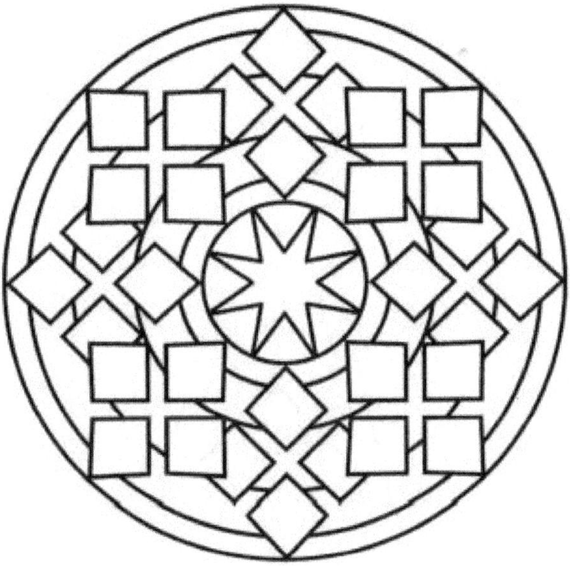

Design 30

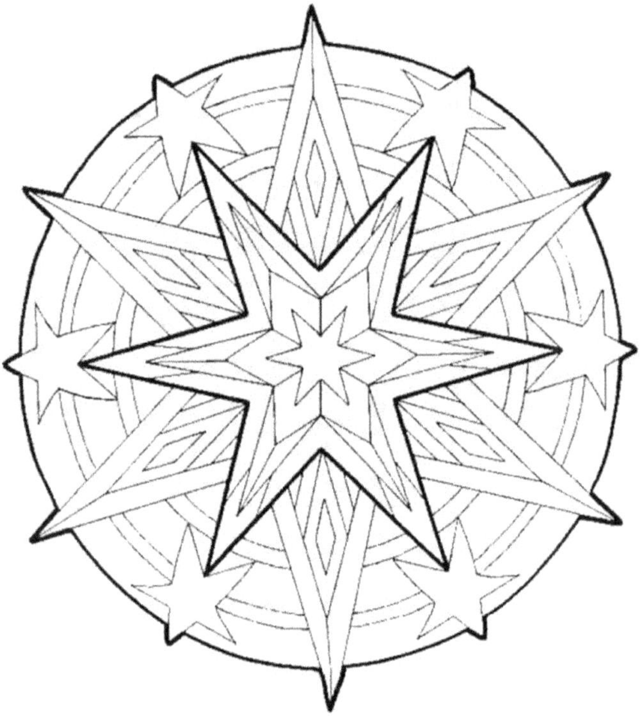

www.ingramcontent.com/pod-product-compliance
Lightning Source LLC
Chambersburg PA
CBHW071557170526
45166CB00004B/1704
9781522707813